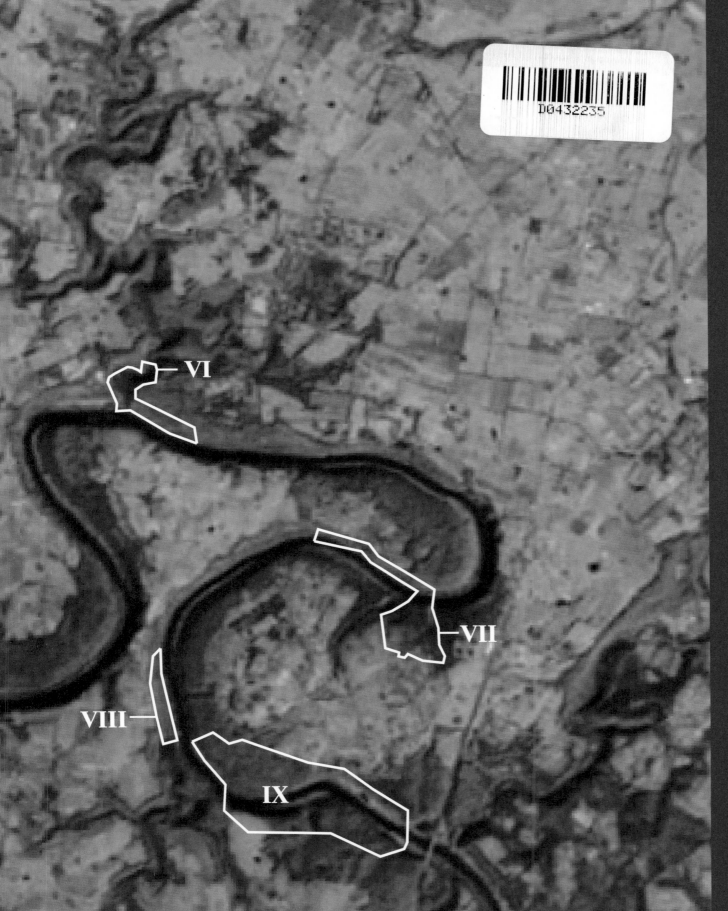

KEY:

- **I** Shaker Village Property on Palisades
- **II** Kentucky River Lock and Dam Seven
- **III** High Bridge Park
- **IV** Kentucky Utilities Property on Dix River
- **V** Sally Brown Nature Preserve (*option*)
- **VI** The Nature Conservancy at Jessamine Creek
- **VII** Jim Beam Nature Preserve
- **VIII** The Nature Conservancy at White Oak Creek
- **IX** Kentucky River Authority at Camp Nelson

25-Meter True Color Image
Palisades Region of the Kentucky River
PREPARED BY THE
KENTUCKY RIVER AUTHORITY

*The Palisades of the
Kentucky River at sunrise.*

Dawn on the Kentucky River.

Jessamine Creek in early spring.

The Palisades
of the Kentucky River

Photography by **Adam Jones**

Foreword by **Barry Bingham, Jr.**

Text by **Richard Taylor**

Sponsored by

KENTUCKY
CHAPTER

ENGLEWOOD, COLORADO

INTERNATIONAL STANDARDS
BOOK NUMBER   1-56579-231-9

PHOTOGRAPHY   © Adam Jones, 1997. All Rights Reserved
TEXT   © Richard Taylor, 1997. All Rights Reserved
INTRODUCTION   © Diana Ratliff, 1997. All Rights Reserved
FOREWORD   © Barry Bingham, Jr., 1997. All Rights Reserved

EDITOR   Sallie M. Greenwood
DESIGN AND COMPOSITION   Rebecca Finkel, F + P Graphic Design
PRODUCTION MANAGER   Harlene Finn

PUBLISHED BY   Westcliffe Publishers, Inc.
2650 South Zuni Street
Englewood, Colorado 80110

PRINTED BY   C & C Offset Printing Co. Ltd.
Printed in Hong Kong

LIBRARY OF CONGRESS
CATALOGING-IN-PUBLICATION DATA

Jones, Adam, 1953–
    The Palisades of the Kentucky River / photo-
graphy by Adam Jones : text by Richard Taylor.
        p.   cm.
    ISBN 1–56579–231–9
    1. Cliffs — Kentucky — Kentucky River.
2. Kentucky River Region (Ky.) — Description
and travel. I. Taylor, Richard, 1941–
II. Title.
F457.K3J66 1997   97–8934
976.9'3 — dc21   CIP

For more information about
other fine books and calendars
from Westcliffe Publishers, please
contact your local bookstore,
write or call (303) 935-0900,
or fax (303) 935-0903 for
our free catalogue.

Table of Contents

*Pollys Bend and Jim Beam Nature Preserve,
Jessamine and Garrard Counties.*

Male northern cardinal among hawthorn berries.

Acknowledgments

After spending a year exploring the Palisades of the Kentucky River by boat, helicopter, on foot, and dangling from ropes, I've developed a deep personal appreciation of the area and a list of many people to thank. First I would like to thank John Fielder of Westcliffe Publishers, and the Kentucky Nature Conservancy for having the confidence in me to complete this project. Jim Aldrich, director, and Julian Campbell, field botanist, for the Kentucky Chapter of the Nature Conservancy were particularly helpful in directing me to the most important areas. By the way, Jim Aldrich deserves a cooking award for his skillet-fried venison cooked on the boat one morning.

I am deeply indebted to Ned Meekins who spent many long hours helping with equipment and ferrying me up and down the river in his boat. Without Ned's knowledge of the river and unwavering support, this book would have been impossible. I would also like to thank my friend Rod Patterson who also shared many of my adventures and to whom I entrusted my life to his expertise with ropes. Thanks above all to the many private landowners who granted me the privilege of photographing their properties.

Finally, I would like to thank my wonderful wife, Sherrie, who makes every day special.

—*Adam Jones*

Acknowledgments

The individuals whose help was valuable in the completion of this project include Dr. Jim Klotter, Kentucky Historical Society; Dr. Thomas D. Clark, Lexington; Hugh Archer and Brian Higgins of the Kentucky River Authority; Charles Parrish, Army Corps of Engineers, Louisville; Susan Hughes, Don Pelly, Tom Edwards, Star Kephart, Bruce and James Herring, Jim Thomas, and Dr. Frank Ettensohn, all associated with Shaker Village of Pleasant Hill; Neal Hammon, Shelbyville; Dr. William Ellis, Eastern Kentucky University; and Charles Hockensmith, Kentucky Heritage Commission. I am especially grateful to my friend Michael Moran, whose editorial eye tamed extravagant phrases and generated good sense. Special thanks to my wife, Lizz, whose tolerance and computer assistance were indispensable.

—*Richard Taylor*

The Kentucky Chapter of the Nature Conservancy gratefully acknowledges the generous contribution of the Commonwealth of Kentucky, Helen Alexander, Sandra Anne Frazier, Mrs. A. B. Hancock, Jr., Mrs. Warner L. Jones, Mr. and Mrs. Rowland Miller, and Maj. Gen. Dillman Rash. Through their interest in conservation, their commitment to preserving the diversity of life on earth, and their respect and fondness for Sally Brown, they have made our dream a stunningly beautiful reality.

Jessamine Creek in autumn.

Foreword

Sally Brown is Kentucky's leading conservationist; she's in the same league with other Titans in the field such as Harry Caudill and Wendell Berry. She joined The Nature Conservancy in 1973, and in 1979 focused the Conservancy's attention on the need to preserve the Palisades of the Kentucky River, to which this book is dedicated. Were it not for her vision and generosity, a substantial piece of land on the Palisades would have never been preserved. Her track record in the field of conservation is not only long and enviable but punctuated with accomplishments that she is too modest to include in her biographical data. For example, she is a founding member of the Kentucky Nature Conservancy and received the Conservancy's highest honor, the Oak Leaf Award, in 1989. She has also received the Frances K. Hutchinson Medal for National Service for conservation, the Garden Club of America's highest award. A 1978 profile of her says, "To Sally Brown conservation is not a hobby or an avocation but a way of life." That is why she has made such a lasting mark as one who would preserve the beauty of God's earth and its creatures and prevent their destruction.

Sally Brown is as driven and determined as any type-A executive you have ever met. If I describe her as a relentless seeker of perfection and achievement, you might not understand that she is also charming, graceful, and often self-effacing.

It is one of life's ironies that people transplanted to Kentucky sometimes see the natural wonders and beauty of our state with clearer eyes than those of us who were born here. That is the case with Sally Brown, who was born in Alaska. The daughter of an officer in the United States Army, Brig. Gen. Martin Shallenberger, she lived in seven states and six foreign countries before settling in Louisville in 1935. Her marriage to W. L. Lyons Brown, of Brown-Forman Distillers Corporation,

Conservationist, Sally Brown

immediately gave her access to all the important people in the Commonwealth. She could easily have devoted herself to the cultivated and pleasant life of society rather than clambering over rocks and through the woods of eastern Kentucky, as well as the rain forests and savannas of Zaire. She has never been content to be a "rocking chair conservationist;" she demands to see the land that has been ravaged by mining, blighted with billboards, or still pristine and available for preservation. She has seen the best and the worst of our state, and she always casts her lot for reclamation of the damaged and preservation of the untrammeled.

Perhaps part of her success is that she rises long before any rooster crows, and she puts in a day's work before most of us push back from the breakfast table. She also possesses a memory that contains more gigabits than today's computers. She knows almost every tree, shrub, and flower in the forest, and not only by its common name. She can (and does) challenge professional botanists with the Latin names of plants and details of their natural venues.

And, while much of her life and energy have been devoted to the world of nature and the nurture thereof, her love of the arts and education is also legendary. Her philanthropy has enriched a wide spectrum of causes, but her money is no more cherished than her guidance. She knows the mark of excellence when she sees it, and she insists that those she helps share her vision. So we of the Kentucky Nature Conservancy bestow tribute to Sally Brown with this book. The words and pictures that follow bring to you the vision of a world she has seen and loves. Her tireless pursuit of uncommon beauty, unblemished land, and uncompromising stewardship provides a model for those of us who follow, in awe, in her footsteps. For all that she is, we dedicate this book to Sally Brown, from Kentucky, with love.

Barry Bingham, Jr.

Kentucky Lady Slipper Orchid

Introduction

The Palisades of the Kentucky River are known to generations of Kentuckians as a scenic landmark. Since 1979 the Kentucky Chapter of The Nature Conservancy, along with scientists from the Kentucky State Nature Preserves Commission, University of Kentucky, Eastern Kentucky University, Thomas More College, Centre College, and Asbury College, has studied the biological importance of the area and targeted key privately owned properties for acquisition for conservation purposes. Remarkably diverse in habitats—including woodlands, patches of prairie, waterfalls, cliffs, and caves—the area supports an abundance of plant and animal life, including many rare and endangered species. Thankfully, much of the fragile ecosystem has remained as it was.

"If I were a painter," wrote nineteenth century wood-block carver Thomas Bewick, "I would go to Nature for all my patterns." His words immediately bring to mind the Palisades with its complex patterns of nature, all having a special niche in Kentucky's web of life.

The Palisades lie at the center of the Inner Bluegrass Region where the Kentucky River cuts through the oldest rock formations exposed in the Commonwealth. The dolomitic limestone forms high palisade cliffs along portions of the river and its tributaries. The river began slowly and persistently cutting through these majestic limestone cliffs between 400,000 and 1 million years ago. In mottled shades of yellows, grays, and whites, the cliffs rise 400 feet above the river in some places, including the Jim Beam Nature Preserve, at Hall, near Camp Nelson. The Conservancy is focusing its efforts to protect the Palisades, especially the section of the Kentucky River from Camp Nelson to Mundy's Landing, a twenty-six-mile section that geologists describe as one of the most extensively entrenched, meandering water systems in the eastern United States.

More than 400 native plant species are found within the Palisades area, along with twenty-five species of mammals, and thirty-six species of reptiles and amphibians. Conservation of the Palisades of the Kentucky River, located only thirty minutes from Lexington, offers the rare opportunity to blend research, education, and sound land management practices to protect a part of Kentucky's startlingly beautiful natural heritage.

The Palisades support the highest concentration of rare plant species within the Bluegrass Region, sheltering such imperiled plants as mountain lover, Svenson's wild-rye, and cleft phlox, all candidates for federal listing as endangered plants. Snow trillium, a member of the lily family, occurs in the shallow limestone soils along the Palisades, otherwise it is unknown anywhere else in Kentucky. The most unusual habitat for vegetation within the Palisades occurs on the rocky river banks, called the scour zone, where there is an abundance of big bluestem, wild oats, riverbank goldenrod, shrubby Saint-John's-wort, and tufted hair grass.

The largest forested areas remaining in the Inner Bluegrass are along the Kentucky River: Beech and yellow poplars (tulip tree) grow tall on terraces and on the banks of its tributaries; species such as blue ash, chinquapin oak, and sugar maple, with a special mixture of rock elm, yellowwood, and yellow buckeye, dominate the steep slopes above the river.

Salamanders washed down from eastern Kentucky on the crests of floods now dwell high above the river and are found nowhere else in central Kentucky. In just one afternoon on the Garrard County portion of the Jim Beam Nature Preserve, a U.S. Forest Service biologist found several rare salamander species in addition to twenty-three species of snails.

Bobcats still roam the more remote portions of the Palisades, and endangered gray and Indiana bats, and the rare Keen's bat inhabit caves along the spectacular cliffs; the only known breeding colony of gray bats in the Bluegrass Region remains in this river corridor. Great blue herons glide over the water, kingfishers perch on branches above the river's edge, and endangered peregrine falcons, recently reintroduced, once again wheel and soar gracefully above the landscape.

Along with The Nature Conservancy, the Kentucky State Nature Preserves Commission, Kentucky River Authority, Kentucky Department of Fish & Wildlife Resources, and the National Fish & Wildlife Foundation are working cooperatively to ensure protection of the Palisades.

Anyone who ever gazed in awe at the towering limestone cliffs understands that the area must be preserved for future generations. The Nature Conservancy's Kentucky Chapter is striving to preserve and to protect the extraordinary natural beauty and diversity of one of Kentucky's true natural wonders.

DIANA RATLIFF
Kentucky Chapter, The Nature Conservancy

White snakeroot atop cliffs at Pollys Bend, Garrard County.

Geology and Natural History

"Among the natural curiosities of this country," writes John Filson in *The Discovery and Settlement of Kentucky,* "the winding banks, or rather precipices of Kentucke, and Dick's Rivers, deserve the first place." Published in 1784, this earliest travel guide to Kentucky country perhaps for the first time records a viewer's response to the natural wonders of the Kentucky River Palisades:

> The astonished eye there beholds almost every where three or four hundred feet of a solid perpendicular lime-stone rock; in some parts a fine white marble, either curiously arched, pillared or blocked up into fine building stones. These precipices are like the sides of a deep trench, or canal; the land above being level, except where creeks set in, and crowned with fine groves of red cedar.

Limestone cliffs, Jessamine Creek Gorge.

More than two centuries later—scarcely a nod in the river's long evolution—these natural geological wonders remain essentially as Filson described them. Writing as a real estate promoter and not as a geologist—geology being at best a rudimentary science at the time—Filson had a sure eye for the unique topography of one of the oldest rivers on the continent. The Kentucky River Palisades, though broken in places, extend nearly 100 miles between Fort Boonesborough State Park and Glenn's Creek, a small tributary a few miles north of Frankfort. Through this gorge the water level is from 300 to 400 feet below the rimrock.

The forces that carved this gorge through Ordovician limestone, the oldest exposed rock formations in Kentucky, comprise a geological saga, a slow though sometimes dramatic evolution of action between stationary rock and moving water.

Running nearly 255 miles, the Kentucky River flows from the confluence of the North, Middle, and South forks at Beattyville in the Cumberland Mountains of eastern Kentucky, generally in a northwesterly course to the Ohio River at Carrollton, a historic river town located midway between Cincinnati and Louisville. At Carrollton—first known as Port William—there is a historic marker that commemorates James McBride, an early explorer who canoed down the Ohio to the mouth of the river and carved his initials and the date, 1754, on a tree that remained a landmark for many years. The Kentucky passes through Frankfort, the state capital, the name of which was derived through mishearing "Frank's Ford." Frank was Stephen Frank, an ill-fated pioneer killed by Indians. More important than the towns and cities along its course is the region through which the river passes—the Bluegrass, the celebrated horse country of Kentucky. Significantly, many cities in the Bluegrass today, including Lexington, are tied to the Kentucky as the primary source of their water.

Contained entirely within Kentucky's borders, the river drains an area of approximately 7,000 square miles and drops 226 feet as it flows from Beattyville to its confluence with the Ohio at Carrollton. The three forks trace their headwaters to the Cumberlands of eastern Kentucky, including the long ridge of Pine Mountain, thus extending the river's true length to 420 miles. Its largest tributaries are the Dix River near Shaker Landing and Elkhorn Creek just north of Frankfort. Larger creeks that feed into the river include Jessamine, Hickman, Boone, Raven, Clear, and Gilbert, many of them forming their own deep cuts or gorges with scenic falls or "step-stone cascades" before spilling into the main stream. According to the Kentucky River Authority, the governmental entity that currently oversees the river, it is home to 377 species of fish and wildlife as well as thirty-one species of

*Kentucky River just east of
U.S. 27 and Camp Nelson.*

*Caves provide habitat for
endangered bat species.*

Jessamine Creek in spring.

Cliffs and eroded rocks, Herrington Lake.

seasonal waterfowl; twenty-five species are listed as threatened or endangered. The objective of The Nature Conservancy and other concerned agencies and individuals is to protect the habitat of these species as well as the more than 400 native plant species that grow here. As Thomas D. Clark, dean of Kentucky historians, says, "the Palisades should be preserved intact as one of Kentucky's most striking landmarks, and as a magnificent stretch of Kentucky's natural scenic beauty…this stretch of the Kentucky River is one of the handsomest features of Kentucky."

Geologically, the Kentucky presents an image both of old age and of youth. According to geologist Dr. Frank Ettensohn of the University of Kentucky, the river in its present course is between 2 and 3 million years old and cuts through and

exposes sedimentary limestone deposited about 450 million years ago. Former state geologist Willard Rouse Jillson, who wrote extensively about the river and its history, theorized that the earliest course of the river was much different than it is now. Following its northwesterly course during the Mesozoic, 200 million years ago to 70 million years ago, long before the Ohio River was formed during the last period of glaciation, the Kentucky may have flowed from what is now North Carolina into what is now Indiana.

In the Miocene Epoch of the mid-Tertiary, 10 to 25 million years ago, the river wound through broad floodplains in what is now central Kentucky. Its sluggishness and meandering were signs of geological senility, but the river underwent a profound change that eventually resulted in the deep gorges we see today. There are several theories to explain how these gorges came to be; two of the most current attribute regional uplift and the dropping of sea level during the early ice ages to causing the gorges.

Regional uplift, a tectonic phenomenon that has occurred in cycles over hundreds of millions of years, raised the Lexington Peneplain, the lowland area that had been gradually reduced to a plain by erosion. The result of lifting the plain 500 or 600 feet was to rejuvenate the area's streams and rivers because gravity now could play a more active role. Along its old course, the young river cut a deeper channel, actively etching the riverbed to form deep gorges within the existing valleys. Physiographic studies indicate that this uplift was in two phases; the first raised the peneplain about 150 feet and formed a floodplain that was moderately wide. The second uplift was cut several hundred feet deeper into the valley floor. The first valley floor formed a kind of terrace below hilltop level and several hundred feet above the present riverbed. Another theory argues that the lowering of sea level as a consequence of glaciation accelerated the process of erosion that cut through the masses of limestone. In some ways fault lines, those fractures in which there has been actual displacement of the sedimentary layers in relation to each other, contributed to the process, because water is able to cut more acutely where there is less resistance as a result of displacement. The winding course of the river crosses the Kentucky River Fault at least nine times. One such fault is plainly visible in the highway cut at Camp Nelson in Jessamine County where U.S. 27 crosses the river.

Cascading water.

Another place to see the fault is at the Clay's Ferry Bridge that joins Fayette and Madison Counties. Here, the river crosses the Kentucky River Fault in two places, and the displacement of sedimentary beds is clearly visible along the old road leading to the bridge.

In an area that has much to please the eye, the most scenic natural attraction is the Kentucky River gorge. It is crossed by more than a half dozen main highways: Kentucky 627 at Boonesboro, Interstate 75 and U.S. 25 at Clay's Ferry, U.S. 27 at Camp Nelson, U.S. 68 at Tyrone and Brooklyn Bridge, and Interstate 64 at Frankfort. Brooklyn Bridge perhaps provides the most impressive prospect of rugged rock formations that do justice to the sense of battlements and walled invulnerability that the name palisades suggests. In many instances bridges such as that at Brooklyn Bridge, replaced ferries that at one time presented the only reliable means of crossing the Kentucky. Ferries in the Palisades area included Shryock's in Woodford County; Curd's Ferry at the mouth of the Dix River at High Bridge; Clay's Ferry in Madison County; Shaker Ferry and Oregon Ferry in Mercer County; and Valley View. The latter joins Fayette and Madison Counties on Kentucky 169 and is the oldest continuously operated business of record in Kentucky, having received its license from Virginia in 1785.

A walk down the face of the Palisades is literally a trip through millions of years of geological time. On a chilly morning in late October at Pleasant Hill, I accompanied a small group of nature lovers on a geological odyssey at the Palisades near Shaker Landing in Mercer County. Our guides were geologist Dr. Frank Ettensohn and Star Kephart, a very knowledgeable, long-time employee of Shaker Village. The descent of several hundred feet from the uplands at the village to the landing crosses several major formations of limestone deposited during the Ordovician (460 million to 445 million years ago) of the Paleozoic era. At the uppermost level the Lexington group of limestones are replete with the fossilized remains of crinoids (sea lilies), gastropods (snails), cephalopods (squid-like creatures), brachiopods (shelled, clam-like creatures), trilobites (extinct marine arthropods), and bryozoans (moss animals). The presence of these life forms indicates that the Bluegrass Region at the time was covered by a shallow inland sea with environmental conditions that Dr. Ettensohn describes as a "sub-tropical paradise." Rich in phosphorous, these rocks account for the region's reputation for lush farmland and ideal conditions for building strong bones in livestock and Thoroughbred horses.

More directly, surface rock has been put to use in other kinds of building. The ubiquitous stone fences at the former Shaker community at Pleasant Hill, or Shaker Village, are constructed mostly of the gray Lexington limestone, though Tyrone limestones, which tend to bleach white, are mixed in, giving some of the stone walls a mottled appearance. As a testament to their sophisticated knowledge of masonry, the Shakers chose to use the whiter, harder Tyrone limestones for the foundations and walls of many of their buildings. When closely examined, their hewn blocks reveal scorings and burrows of sea creatures millions of years old.

Continuing the descent to the Shaker Landing road, we pass through the Tyrone and then the Oregon formations, calcified sedimentary beds largely formed by carbonate mud. This mud hardened into stones scored with the spoors and burrows of creatures that flourished in an environment similar to today's tidal marshes in Georgia or South Carolina. Referred to as trace fossils, these streaks and burrows are etched in the rock, in some places displaying a honeycomb effect with thousands of pittings on the rock faces. Many of these laminate formations were the result of thin layers of sediment laid down in tidal flats where thin skims of water covered the muds in which these burrowing creatures left their mark. In places there are outcroppings of bentonite, a clay formed by the decomposition of volcanic ash that blew in from the east and settled in the area. The steep, nearly vertical cliffs of the Palisades form a perfect window into the ages, making the descent at Shaker Landing like beachcombing through time.

Though the vertical is revealing, it is hard to get a visual sense of the continuity of the Palisades because there is no paved road and few pathways that parallel the river for any distance. The most accessible and safest point from which to view the rocky facades is the river itself. During the warmer months of the year, Shaker Village of Pleasant Hill runs an excursion boat from Shaker Landing along a mile or so of the river over one of its most impressive stretches. For the price of a ticket one can experience the river as the first settlers saw it—a narrow strip of sky between two steeply wooded and rocky cliffs that form a picturesque and rugged gorge several hundred feet below the rolling Bluegrass farmland of Mercer and Jessamine Counties.

Central to the formation of the Palisades is the High Bridge limestone, formed during the Middle Ordovician period, from 440 million to 500 million years ago. The oldest rocks surfacing in Kentucky, they form a part of the Cincinnati Arch, the domelike formation of central Kentucky that Jillson describes as "an arrested uplift of mountain-making proportions." He writes in *The Kentucky River,* that the Cincinnati Arch has exposed "the oldest strata at the point of greatest uplift." Because

Stream and moss-covered rocks.

Stone fence and work horses,
Mercer County.

Morning fog lingers above the Kentucky River, Jessamine County.

Morning along a tree-lined drive,
Jessamine County.

this stone is so hard, it is slower to erode than the more soluble stone around it, and Jillson states that, "the exposed hard rocks in the Kentucky river valley are limestones, dolomitic limestones, sandstones and shales of Devonian, Silurian, and Ordovician age." One of the most readable accounts of the geological evolution of the river is Mary E. Wharton's and Roger W. Barbour's *Bluegrass Land and Life* published in 1991:

> The Kentucky River in its meandering course had massive-bedded, resistant rock to cut into
> as it passed through what we now call the Inner Bluegrass. Hence today it is characterized by
> entrenched meanders: a sinuous, old-age course that developed on a low plain, now incised
> and confined between rock walls. Such entrenched meanders are relatively rare throughout
> the world.

The gorge itself is discontinuous because it crosses the Kentucky River Fault system several times. Because of displacement along these faults, the erosion of resistant rocks of the High Bridge group are below drainage level in several places. The result is wider valleys and gradual slopes that replace the vertical cliffs of the gorge. In places there are gently wooded slopes and floodplains that are wide enough to farm.

The dramatic rock formations and wild aspect make the river and Palisades the beauty spot of the Bluegrass. Among the natural curiosities are formations like Candlestick Rock, an isolated column of limestone on a bluff near Camp Nelson, upstream from High Bridge, that is an example of differential erosion. Almost equally impressive is the gorge of the Dix River, the Kentucky's largest tributary. Most of this gorge, however, has been flooded since 1925 when the Dix River Dam, the largest rock-filled dam east of the Mississippi River, was completed to form thirty-five-mile-long Herrington Lake and to produce hydroelectric power; this is also the site of another chimney or candlestick rock, now partially submerged.

What we see along the Palisades, as Wharton and Barbour point out, is the result of geological processes, a natural tension of construction and destruction that represents a phase in the long planetary process of flattening what rises through erosion:

> The present topography has developed since the Pliocene uplift (4 or 5 million years ago):
> the river cutting a gorge, tributaries downcutting to a lesser extent, and sinks and caves
> developing in the inter stream uplands as rainwater dissolves some of the limestone. The
> new cycle of erosion has not progressed far because downcutting into the resistant massive
> High Bridge limestone by the Kentucky River, the master stream, and its immediate
> tributaries has necessarily been slow.

Glaciation during the Pleistocene had no direct effect on the area because glaciers did not extend farther south than the Ohio River. This factor has a great bearing on the area's topography. The beauty of the Inner Bluegrass, which is surrounded by three discontinuous arcs of slightly more rolling terrain—the Outer Bluegrass—that extends to a fringe of hilly knobs, consists mostly of gently rolling land, neither hilly nor level, that forms a low plateau.

Kentucky countryside.

Flora and Fauna

Harry Toulmin, a transplanted Englishman, was among the first to make specific reference to the flora of the region. "The rivers," he wrote, in his 1792 *A Description of Kentucky in North America,* "have the appearance of deep, artificial canals. Their banks are level, and covered with red-cedar groves." About the same time, in 1793, the great French naturalist André Michaux made these notes in his *Journal of Travels in Kentucky:*

> Crossed the Kentucky river the banks of which are very close to one another… On arriving there one would think himself between two ranges of very steep Mountains but in fact it is merely a torrent or a river whose Bed has been deeply worn. The rocks on the banks are of a calcareous nature. Several shrubs and Plants, natives of Carolina, grow on the cliff with a southern exposure, being secured and protected from cold by the favorable situation offered by the great depth of the river.

A more recent and authoritative description of plant communities in the gorge area is Wharton's and Barbour's *Bluegrass Land and Life.* Combining their years of study, Mary Wharton as a botanist and Roger Barbour as a zoologist and photographer inventoried plants typically growing in the Palisades region. As might be expected, the variety of vegetation along the Palisades is great, given the dramatic range of available habitats along the slopes and cliffs above the river. Beginning on the riverbank, the habitats are sorted by tiers. Just above water level (and sometimes under it) the dominant tree is water maple, though box elder, sycamore, and elm are also represented. In some places elderberry forms a shrub layer. Floodplains have usually been cleared for homesites or cultivated fields. Those that have returned to woodland consist largely of sycamore, water maple, box elder, and elm, as well as black walnut and shellbark hickory. The occasional beech or white bass adds some variety. The shrub layer consists of pawpaw, spicebush, and elderberry.

Talus at the base of the cliffs supports a mix of hackberry, Kentucky coffee trees, black walnut, sugar maple, buckeye, and butternuts among its rocks, as well as smaller representations of red mulberry, great shellbark hickory, and black cherry.

The steep slopes are forested, though broken in places by exposed rock cliffs. Most have been logged, and because the soil tends to be shallow, the trees are of smaller size. For the same reason, their purchase often is tenuous since root systems are not as deep. According to Wharton and Barbour, forests on the steepest slopes are of the mixed mesophytic—plants that require a medium amount of moisture—the type associated with eastern Kentucky, with combinations of maple-oak-ash as well as oak-hickory-cedar. The combinations depend largely on soil depth, exposure, and moisture. The understory includes dogwood, black haw, hornbeam, yellowwood, bladdernut, and spicebush.

The summits, where the soil is thin and dry, support red cedar, and the earliest explorers found communities of red cedars existing in groves, the habitat being too harsh for species needing more moisture. Other trees found atop the cliffs include oak, hickory, and ash with an understory of redbud, bittersweet, and aromatic sumac.

The earliest life forms of the gorge area, embedded in stone, date to when shallow seas covered the area more than 400 million years ago. The sediment of these seas eventually hardened into rock and contain fossilized marine life. Salt licks not

Endangered snow trillium.

Coneflowers along the shoreline
of the Dix River, Mercer County.

Above: Autumn leaves, Mercer County.

Left: Elk Lick Creek.

A carpet of blue-eyed Marys.

far from the Kentucky yielded the remains of now-extinct mammals that date to the last period of glaciation and cover a period between 9,000 and 10,000 years ago. At Big Bone Lick in Boone County diggers have unearthed the remains of mastodons, mammoths, giant sloths, bison, primitive horses, musk oxen, moose, and caribou. In the foyer of Monticello, President Thomas Jefferson's home in Virginia, are the bones of extinct Pleistocene mammals fetched from the licks in 1807 by explorer Captain William Clark, who had rendered great service in the Far West a few years earlier. Jefferson, arguably the country's first archaeologist, had an insatiable curiosity about the western country and the extinct life forms it rendered up for study. The licks and area caves also contain the remains of extinct species of bison, elk, deer, and bear. Evidence indicates that 13,000 years ago central Kentucky was a vast boreal semiprairie or parkland with the ancient river cutting through its center.

At the time of the white incursion into the river valley, the region was a hunter's paradise. The Long Hunters, so called because they traveled great distances and for extended periods, found enormous herds of bison whose traces formed a network through the Bluegrass, crossing the Kentucky at Frankfort and proceeding to salt licks where mammals, large and small, came to satisfy their craving for salt. These buffalo roads, some of them cutting a swath forty feet wide through the countryside, formed the basis of Kentucky's first highway system. Historian Ted Belue in *The Long Hunt* chronicled the senseless slaughter of the herds from 1750 onward. Sometimes they were shot for food or hides, but more often those who killed them were wasteful and excessive, so that by 1800 bison in Kentucky had virtually been eliminated. The same is true nearly a century later for the passenger pigeon, which literally obliterated the sky in its migratory flights. A friend's grandfather who lived in Frankfort just before the turn of the century swore that the pigeons were so plentiful they blackened the sun for three days as they passed over the river valley. In 1914 the last one died in captivity in the Cincinnati Zoo. Preserving the river basin is key to protecting the richness of the area's surviving plant and animal communities.

Hepatica, a sure sign of spring, Jessamine County.

Wild hyacinth and wood poppy.

A painted lady on
a black-eyed Susan.

*Lady ferns and a purple fringed orchid,
near Pine Mountain, headwaters
of the Kentucky River.*

Hickory horned devil caterpillar,
metamorphoses into a royal walnut moth.

Virginia bluebells,
Jessamine Creek Gorge.

White dogwood in fog,
Jessamine County.

*Cliffs and spring foliage,
Jessamine Creek Gorge.*

Autumn, Jessamine County.

Human History

From the earliest times the Kentucky River has served as a corridor into the rich hunting lands through which it flows in its journey to the Ohio. Winding in a northwesterly course, the river passes from the rugged uplands of southeastern central Kentucky to the fabled Bluegrass with the fertile soil and lush vegetation that for millennia supported an abundance of wildlife, including bison, turkeys, deer, and bears, as well as numerous species of small game. Only recently have humans appeared in this natural paradise. Though no permanent village has survived into historic times, archaeological evidence indicates that the river had been used extensively by prehistoric peoples. Paleo-Indians, ancestors of the Native Americans, floated on this natural highway for thousands of years. Since trails were few and loads limited to what a strong back could carry, streams and rivers became a primary means among these migratory peoples for transporting their possessions and food. These realities account for the evidence of early settlements and camps along rivers and their tributaries.

Along most of the state's waterways, including the Kentucky, archaeologists have discovered earthen mounds, great heaps transported to specific sites for purposes still being debated. Some mounds were used for burials or other ceremonial purposes while others were constructed more practically for defense. A large stone fortification, popularly known as Indian Fort, stands three miles east of Berea in Madison County, at the head of Silver Creek, which empties into the Kentucky opposite Jessamine County. Built by prehistoric people atop a steep and rugged mountain, the elaborate stonework of this stronghold encompasses between 400 and 500 acres and would have controlled access to what is now known as the Bluegrass Region.

A more typical prehistoric site is the Capitol View Site, a small, semicircular settlement on a narrow ridge in south-central Franklin County a little over a mile from the river and within sight of the present state capitol. Occupied circa A.D. 1400 for no longer than a decade, the community consisted of about seventy individuals who resided in eight structures and lived by farming and hunting. They supplemented domesticated crops such as corn, beans, and sunflowers with such wild fruits as sumac, grapes, blackberries, raspberries, and plums, as well as several varieties of nuts. Their diet of meat, more varied than our own, included venison, bear, elk, bison, and wild turkey, as well as smaller animals such as bobcat, raccoon, squirrel, opossum, skunk, rabbit, and muskrat. The river supplied turtles, fish, and freshwater

A sycamore and autumn colors, Handys Bend, Jessamine County.

mussels. Among the artifacts unearthed at the site are ceramic fragments of a hand-modeled spoon or ladle, a tiny figurine, and a ceramic disk, in addition to more commonplace jars, pans, and bowls. These people and others living in the area before and after them had the Palisades as their backyard.

Abandoned barn along the Kentucky River, Jessamine County.

Dawn on the Kentucky River.

Early saxifrage,
Jessamine Creek Gorge.

Above: Eastern cottontail,
Jessamine County.

Right: Fence and buggy shed,
Jessamine County.

A farm, Inner Bluegrass Region.

Young red fox.

A barn and historic High Bridge at Shaker Landing.

What the First Settlers Saw

In the east nave of the Kentucky State Capitol at Frankfort is a mural by Gilbert White of explorer Daniel Boone and buckskin-clad companions taking their first view of what John Filson's Boone describes as "the beautiful level of Kentucke." Though historically this event occurred at Pilot Knob miles to the east, the artist has placed Boone on a high bluff overlooking what is now the city of Frankfort, the state capital. Significantly, the point from which he gazes is his own monument in the Frankfort Cemetery. Its limestone, called Kentucky marble, was quarried from strata found at Fort Boonesborough, the earliest white settlement on the Kentucky River. Prominent in the painting is a wide curve of the river and a panorama of the high bluffs that dominate the river valley. The image combines an impressive vista of land and water, the four figures frozen as if anticipating the rush of immigration that is soon to follow. They pause, contemplating a natural beauty that in most of Kentucky that is west of the Appalachians will be transformed by ax and rifle. The river valley that they survey, particularly the Palisades that extend from Frankfort a hundred miles or so upriver to Boone's fort, is fixed in a timeless tableau of water-sculpted rock, a treasure house of natural beauty and wildlife that has defied

A pair of peregrine falcons reintroduced to the region by the Kentucky Utilities Company.

development and despoilment. Like Boone and the capitol dome, the river and its Palisades have become defining icons in the collective identity of Kentuckians.

Kentucky from the first was celebrated for its natural beauty. To give the faithful a vision of their heavenly home, Elijah Craig, who combined his Baptist ministry with whisky making, made heaven a metaphor of Kentucky: "O my dear honeys," he declared, "heaven is a Kentucky of a place." Less Edenic in his descriptions but equally expansive, John Filson, real estate promoter and author of the first book about the Kentucky country, referred to the region transected by the Kentucky as "the best tract of land in North America and probably the world." At its center lay the Kentucky River Basin, incorporating 4.4 million acres of land in what are now forty of Kentucky's 120 counties.

To restless frontiersmen, the vastness through which the Kentucky flowed was an uncharted wilderness. In many places, especially the river valleys, it was a mixed deciduous hardwood forest of oak, hickory, poplar, beech, chestnut, ash, and maple. In others it was an extended, rolling meadow with a skyline that was broken by a few species of fire-resistant trees. Much of the Inner Bluegrass was a savanna, an open grassland dotted with towering giants like the blue ash and burr oak. There were numerous brakes of cane, nearly impenetrable growths, where the stalks were often twelve to fifteen feet high. Extensively watered with streams and rivers, the area contains more miles of streams than any state in the contiguous United States.

Such trails as existed were those used by Indians, many of them following traces carved by bison that migrated in search of pasturage and salt from the numerous licks, or sulphur springs, in central and northern Kentucky. One such buffalo trace between what is now Maysville and Lexington became the easiest and arguably the safest means for travelers from the east to enter into the fertile expanse of central Kentucky. Before it became the Kentucky, the river was variously known by the first white hunters and explorers as the Chenoa, the Cuttawa, and the Louisa or Levisa.

Among the first whites to encounter the Kentucky were the Long Hunters. The Long Hunter best known to Kentuckians is Daniel Boone (1734–1820), Kentucky's and perhaps the nation's most celebrated pioneer. In the summer of 1769 Boone, John Finley, Boone's brother-in-law John Stewart, and several others hunted along the Kentucky in what was then Shawnee hunting grounds. During this six-month-long trip they ascended one of the conical knobs, which gave the muralist his subject and John Filson, Boone's first biographer, an opportunity to commemorate the moment in his "Adventures of Col. Daniel Boone," which appeared in *The Discovery and Settlement of Kentucky.* Filson wrote that the river was "amazingly crooked, upwards of two hundred miles in length, and about one hundred and fifty yards broad."

By 1773 the era of the Long Hunters was passing as land-hungry settlers and speculators from Virginia and Pennsylvania pressed to acquire land in the fertile area drained by the Kentucky. That summer a flotilla of surveyors from Virginia

*Aerial view of the Kentucky River
Palisades and the Jim Beam Nature
Preserve at Pollys Bend.*

Winter view of a tributary,
Jessamine Creek, Jessamine County.

came down the Ohio. One party, the brothers James and Robert McAfee and surveyor Hancock Taylor, left their main camp at Big Bone Lick, and followed the Kentucky River south from the salt lick at Drennon's Springs to the present site of Frankfort. In the wide bottomland of what is now Kentucky's capital they made surveys near the natural ford where the great buffalo trail crossed the Kentucky. Surveying parties were back the next spring under Col. John Floyd, who camped for a time at the mouth of the Kentucky before going up the river about a hundred miles to a point where James Harrod was building "a kind of town."

In 1775 Richard Henderson, a lawyer and entrepreneur who came to Kentucky from North Carolina, attempted to make an independent colony out of part of the Kentucky country. He organized the Louisa Company to purchase a "large territory or tract of land on the Western waters from the Indian tribes." He then reorganized the company as the Transylvania Company and employed Daniel Boone to negotiate with the Cherokee for purchase of the land. On March 17, 1775, at the Watauga River in Tennessee, the parties formed the Treaty of Sycamore Shoals. Under this agreement much of what is now western and central Kentucky, embracing land that lay south of the Kentucky River, was ceded to Henderson for the equivalent of £2,000 sterling in trade goods. Though a Cherokee named Dragging Canoe warned that whites would find Kentucky "a dark and bloody ground," Boone took on the hazardous and back-breaking task of clearing a suitable road into the territory. The Wilderness Road that he and and his road cutters carved extended from Cumberland Gap in the southeastern tip of present-day Kentucky to the Kentucky River near its juncture with Otter Creek in what is now Madison County. There Boone founded the settlement and fort of Boonesborough.

Forts Boonesborough and Harrod, Kentucky's two oldest settlements, both were wholly or partly oriented toward the river. When Boone first reached the valley with his road crew, he saw a multitude of buffalo, "the cattle of a thousand hills," resting under towering sycamores. Having lost three men to Indian attacks on the way to the site, Boone, speaking through biographer John Filson, reports that his party "proceeded on to the Kentucky river without opposition; and on the first day of April (1775) began to erect the fort of Boonsborough at a salt lick, about 60 yards from the river, on the south side."

Henderson envisioned the town that would grow from this fort as the capital of a colony to be named Transylvania. Near the fort under an enormous elm tree, later called the Divine Elm, the first Christian religious services in Kentucky were held. There Henderson and his followers also enacted some of the first laws and a compact recognizing the proprietary rights of the Transylvania Company. Virginia, which had a prior claim to the Kentucky country, finally invalidated the sale and reasserted its dominion over the area. In the fall of 1778, during the American Revolution, the fort withstood a siege of ten days by a force of British and Indians who fired so many musket balls that 125 pounds of lead were later extracted from the stockade walls. The nearby river was also the site of the kidnapping of Daniel Boone's daughter and the Callaway girls (all later recovered) by a small band of Shawnee and Cherokee. Today, despite a nearby quarry, a pavilion, parking lots, and a cluster of buildings that are part of Fort Boonesborough State Park, one can imagine how the area looked when Boone first saw it—the river, a mesh of trees, the high bluffs to the north of the river forming a kind of protective wall. The palisaded reproduction of the original fort, built now on higher ground, features period artifacts and demonstrations of pioneer crafts.

Though Harrodsburg is eight or so miles from the Kentucky, the river played an important role in its formation and later commerce. In 1774 James Harrod and his men came up the Kentucky to Shawnee Run where they traveled overland to erect their fort, the oldest permanent settlement in the state. Some months later, Englishman Nicholas Cresswell succinctly described his approach to Fort Harrod from the river: "June 4th, 1775, arrived at Hardwoods [sic] Landing in the evening. Saw a rattle snake about four feet long. A bark canoe at the Landing… Rocky and Cedar hills along the banks of the river."

From the earliest days a hunter's trace ran from the fort to the mouth of Shawnee Run, which lies in present-day Mercer County. The trace then crossed the river into Jessamine County at Indian Creek, which runs between the rocky cliffs of the Palisades. According to historian George Morgan Chinn, who on occasion quarried Kentucky marble, as the limestone is called, said that Indians once reached a camp in the recesses of the cliffs by following the creek to throw off their pursuers. Even after the Revolution ended, parties of Indians conducted raids until as late as 1793.

Coyote resting in winter.

Red-tailed hawk.

Autumn colors reflected on the Kentucky River.

Historic Mundy's Landing,
Woodford County.

The Shaker Presence

The Kentucky's potential as a means of transporting goods was recognized from the earliest times of white settlement. General James Wilkinson, who came to the Kentucky country in 1783 and laid out what was to become its capital city, first acted on the trade potential of shipping Kentucky products downriver. Choosing Frankfort as his base, he planned to build a commercial empire, using the river to connect Kentucky with the port of New Orleans on the Mississippi. Working with Estaban Miro, the Spanish governor of New Orleans, Wilkinson in 1787 set up an agreement under which Kentucky farmers could profitably ship their products downriver to New Orleans. Wilkinson led the way, arranging for a cargo of tobacco, hams, and butter to be loaded onto a flatboat at the mouth of the Dix River and shipped to Louisville and thence to New Orleans. Markets were suddenly opened for Kentuckians to exploit the profitable southern trade.

Perhaps the most noteworthy group to capitalize on the river trade was a little-known sect called the Society of Believers, or simply, Shakers. As an offshoot of the English Quakers of the eighteenth century, the Shakers believed in celibacy, human perfectibility, and communal living. Their beliefs were utopian, their pastoral environment idyllic. The name derives from Shaking Quakers, the practice of dancing literally to shake sin from their bodies. At the core of their community was a strong entrepreneurial impulse, a practical and tempered capitalism that had its roots in agrarianism and ideals of self-sufficiency.

What became the Shaker settlement at Pleasant Hill started in 1805 on the 140-acre farm of convert Elisha Thomas. It was located on Shawnee Run, a creek that empties through a picturesque wooded ravine into the Kentucky in sight of the towering Palisades. Julia Neal who wrote *The Shakers of Kentucky* included a letter written in December 1807 by an anonymous Shaker at Shawnee Run to the parent Shaker community at New Lebanon, New York, describing the community that was forming in Kentucky:

> The spot where we live is not quite so even as we could wish, yet it is not mountainous…. We are situated on a river by the name of Kentucky river which a considerable part of the year is navigable for boats for about one hundred and forty or fifty miles from its mouth where it empties into the Ohio. The Believers' land is bounded by it on the east, our house stands about three quarters of a mile from it. Up this river there is a number of banks of stone coal, the same with sea coal, which they bring down in boats for blacksmithing and other uses.

A generation after Wilkinson opened the way, the United Brethren of Believers in Christ's Second Appearing had established a utopian community at Pleasant Hill that lasted 105 years and became a part of one of the most successful social experiments in nineteenth century America.

Owning land that afforded access to the river, they quickly looked to the Kentucky as a means of transporting their goods to markets far removed from their tiny enclave. Historian Thomas Clark wrote in his 1942 work on the river, *The Kentucky*, that, to the Shaker's

Shaker handiwork: seed storage containers.

Buggy in barn.

Right: Shaker-made wooden rakes.

Opposite: Farm implements at Pleasant Hill

The Centre Family Dwelling
at Shaker Village of Pleasant Hill.

the river was a kindred spirit. They loved its beautiful green current, and its deep swale. It was an active partner in their dream of perfectionist living. On its current valuable cargoes of farm products were shipped to market, and useful building timber was brought downstream. The river was the connecting link between the Shaker in his realm of spirituality and the "world" which he in reality loved.

But the rough terrain and formidable cliffs of the Palisades made access to the river difficult. In 1786 John Curd had established Curd's Ferry across the river at the mouth of Dick's River, named in 1770 to honor a Cherokee chief, Captain Dick; the river is now known as the Dix. Though the ferry was in operation about a half mile from their land, the brethren wanted a closer site over which they would have full control. The course they decided on was an old horse path that wound around the rock facings. In 1826 they began cutting a first road down to the river. Laboring by hand with picks, shovels, and spud bars, they widened the path to a wagon road for a distance of a mile or so between Pleasant Hill and the river.

Nearly three decades later, they undertook another road-building project. To improve access to the river still more, they purchased another tract, blasting a point off the Palisades to form a second road along the shoulder of the bluff down to their landing, a project begun in 1854 and not completed until 1861. Crews of Irish laborers assisted them in shoveling and hauling tons of displaced rock. Holes bored by their drills are still visible in the rock facings along the road.

An entry from a Shaker journal that Howard Curry included in *High Bridge, A Pictorial History*, recounts the pride of the community in completing this lifeline to the river: "We have undertaken to make a new road over the cliff and all who have seen it, both Believers and the world, say they never saw, nor before thought that a road could be made half as well over such a cliff." This road brought increased local traffic and a steady stream of steamboats to the wharf. The world had come to the Shakers.

For more than half a century Shaker trade on the river, though disrupted by the Civil War, generally thrived, but the completion of vital routes for the railroad in the 1870s marked the beginning of the end of its river-borne prosperity. A combination of other forces—economic, political, and social—added to the momentum. The turning point came during the war years.

Though the Shaker community reached a peak population of 500 in the 1830s, trade slackened as the number of converts declined and the adult population aged. With the Civil War, shipments to New Orleans, their principal market, virtually ceased as the Union blockaded the Mississippi and Southern river ports. And equally damaging, the Union army and the Confederate army routinely imposed on the Shakers, who were pacifists, to feed their troops and horses. By the time the last member of the community died in 1923, the river trade had all but disappeared.

Camp Nelson

Farther upriver from Pleasant Hill, in Jessamine County at the mouth of Hickman Creek, lies Camp Nelson. During the Civil War it was the principal Kentucky center for recruiting and preparing free blacks and former slaves for service in the Union army. Formed in 1863 and named in honor of Major General William "Bull" Nelson, the camp eventually trained over 5,000 U.S. black troops, accounting for two of every five Kentucky black soldiers in the service. Because Kentucky-born President Abraham Lincoln's 1863 Emancipation Proclamation freed only slaves in Confederate states, many Kentucky slaves enlisted to gain their freedom. Thousands of refugees, sometimes 400 a day, poured into the camp. Commandants sometimes turned away those seeking refuge from their white masters. In November 1864 nearly 100 of 400 forced out of the camp froze to death along the road to Nicholasville.

The site of the camp was chosen partially because of the Palisades, which formed an almost impregnable natural defense against attack from the river. Its fortified circumference was about ten miles and included seven forts with cannon emplacements; earthen breastworks completed the defenses of the high hills and cliffs. To prevent Confederate forces from crossing the river and then attacking Camp Nelson from the rear, the defenders built Fort Bramlette atop the Palisades overlooking the river. Another reason for the camp's location was its access to the river, which served as a major route for munitions and supplies throughout the war.

Above: Cleft phlox grow on a dry, rock outcrop.

Opposite: Kentucky River Palisades in early spring.

More than a fort and training ground, Camp Nelson became a community for thousands of refugees, many of them women and children, who flocked to the camp to escape slavery. Substantial frame cottages were erected to replace the tent city that had formed on the grounds, and barracks were constructed to house the troops. Other buildings sheltered supplies, artillery, and wagons. The post had a 700-bed military hospital, which treated wounded Union soldiers. Army engineers devised an elaborate water-supply system to raise water from the river level by a steam pump to fill the camp's large reservoir.

The Reverend John Fee, an evangelical abolitionist, came to Camp Nelson in 1864 and founded a church and a preparatory school for the dependents of soldiers stationed there. Fee described the young enlistees whom he met as "a class of men… which promises great good to this nation." His work at Camp Nelson was an early effort in Kentucky to assimilate ex-slaves and to prepare them for full citizenship. The college that he formed at nearby Berea in 1866 was the first in Kentucky to admit black students.

Camp Nelson today is a quiet community with few buildings remaining from its heyday during the Civil War, the covered bridge built twenty-five years before the camp was established—the first to cross the Kentucky and much used during the Civil War—was razed in 1933. Those of the original buildings not destroyed by floods have either fallen from neglect or were used by local farmers in building other structures. The community was by-passed when U.S. 27 was widened and a new and higher bridge replaced the old one. Unchanged is its national cemetery, which contains the graves of more than 5,000 Union soldiers.

A spiderweb glistens at sunrise.

Old U.S. 27 crosses the historic iron bridge at Camp Nelson.

Above: A hackberry, at sunset in winter.

Left: Camp Nelson National Cemetery.

High Bridge

The construction of High Bridge on a right-of-way sold by Shakers to railroad interests marked a new phase of transportation in central Kentucky. Railways over the next decades steadily eroded the river trade. In sight of Shaker Ferry and downstream from the confluence of the Dix River, the bridge, referred to as "the wonder of Kentucky" during the nineteenth century, is still the most prominent engineering landmark along the Kentucky. When completed in 1877, it was, at 275 feet above the river, the highest bridge in North America and the highest railroad bridge in the world. It connects the Palisades on both sides and has three 375-foot spans that rest on two enormous piers. Stone towers against the Palisades were all that remained of an 1850s attempt by engineer John A. Roebling, who had successfully spanned the Niagara at Niagara Falls in 1855, to build a bridge on the site. Commissioned by the Lexington & Danville Railroad, the first bridge was left incomplete when the railroad failed, a victim of an ailing national economy. Opened in 1877, this second bridge was designed by Charles Shaler Smith and built by the Baltimore Bridge Company

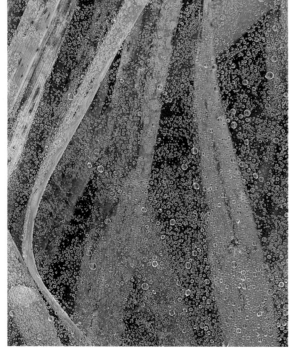

Dew on blades of grass and a sheet web.

for the Cincinnati Southern. Using the most scientific bridge engineering of the time, Shaler Smith employed a cantilever design, the first of its kind in the United States.

To carry heavier loads, the bridge was rebuilt in 1911, using stronger and more resilient steel to gird the earlier ironworks. To prevent rail traffic from being interrupted during construction, the work progressed in such a way that the new bridge was built over and around the old. Only after the new span was completed was the old dismantled. Double tracks were added in the 1920s, and it was not unusual to see trains from opposite directions passing over its span because twenty to thirty trains passed over the bridge daily.

Now designated as a national historic civil engineering landmark, the bridge area on the Jessamine County side was the site of a park and picnic grounds where people made excursions from Cincinnati and central Kentucky to socialize in the last quarter of the nineteenth century. At least one published collection of vintage photographs depicts the bridge, train station, post office, the park, and classic shots of the Palisades. Hundreds of sightseers came by way of the Cincinnati Southern Railway on round-trip tickets costing a dollar. Many of the picnickers and sightseers descended the elaborate stairway of 271 steps, built against the face of the Palisades, to inspect the formations and understructure of the bridge.

Since much of the river valley is inaccessible except by water, perhaps the best way to see the Palisades is aboard the *Dixie Belle,* the double-decker excursion boat in use at Shaker Landing for much of the year. On a beautiful September afternoon my ten-year-old daughter Julia and I bought tickets, finding a seat on the upper deck where we watched the wildness pass us and listened to the pilot, Bruce Herring of Harrodsburg, as he helped us see and understand what we were witnessing. We traveled a mile or so upriver to an area that, aside from several river houses, was untouched by human presence. During that beautiful late afternoon, we were passed by only one boat, a motorboat with two occupants who were sightseeing or perhaps on their way to a favorite fishing spot. They could not have come far because there are no marinas to gas up and few places to put in. Since, like their forefathers, they must carry everything they need, there are limits. This sense of limits, this dwarfing of human dominance under the towering rocks, accounts for much of the Palisades's appeal. After the motorboat had passed, its wake nudged the *Dixie Belle* once or twice before the river composed itself once again.

Over the hum of the engine, Captain Bruce Herring, a young man who obviously loves the river, gave an interesting and informal history of the Kentucky, complete with observations of more immediate flora and fauna along the way: the high

High Bridge spans the Kentucky River.

The Dixie Bell, *a stern-wheeler,*
on the Kentucky River.

*Confluence of the
Dix and Kentucky Rivers.*

A cascade from limestone cliffs
along the Kentucky River.

wheeling of five or six turkey buzzards, the lower transecting flight of a belted kingfisher, the purposeful winging of a red-tailed hawk. Turtles, some as wide as dinner plates, sunned on snags along the bank. When the boat violated their solitude, they simply slid off into the depths. The walls of timber and rock provide a sense of what Native Americans and the Long Hunters witnessed as they paddled the Kentucky in their dugouts. It is possible, here, to experience pristine nature, a green world visually undefiled by cars, billboards, and litter. At one point the captain had us gaze halfway up the steep slopes where we could just discern a white plume of water pouring down an overhang. Over the millennia, he explained, this spring-fed waterfall had deposited lime sediment that formed a "petrified waterfall," a cousin of the stalagmites formed underground in caves.

Relaxing in the sunlight, we journeyed through time. We imagined the log rafts and coal barges that plied the river, conveying the vast resources of eastern Kentucky to lines of transportation at Frankfort and beyond. We could imagine steamboats like the *Blue Wing* of Frankfort cautiously making its way upstream, scraping over the shoals and paddling comfortably through the intervening pools. Stretching, we could almost visualize the river without humans, an immeasurable period that makes up the bulk of its unwritten history. Then we reencounter the most persistent reminder of human presence in the awesome span of High Bridge, especially when a minuscule freight train, not much larger than a Popsicle stick, crosses against the sky above the chasm, which must from above appear a narrow green ribbon of water. A second reminder of our own era came as we approached the mouth of the Dix River. Upstream was Dix Dam, constructed in the 1920s to impound water for hydroelectric power and incidentally to form Herrington Lake, a center of water recreation with camps and cottages around its perimeter.

A frog amid duckweed.

Above: A great blue heron fishes along the shore.

Left: Foggy morning along the Dix River.

*Overhanging branches create
an intricate pattern.*

The South Fork headwaters of the Kentucky River.

Through the Eyes of Others

If not everyone wishes to hike or cruise the length of the gorge area, one must rely on seeing the Palisades through the eyes of others. Most of the available images are photographs, some well over a hundred years old, shot both by amateurs and professionals drawn to the magnificence of the limestone and dolomite gorges. In many of these views High Bridge and the Palisades form a backdrop for Victorian matrons and misses at family outings, got up in white dresses and accompanied by gallused and mustachioed gentlemen posing against the rock facings that bristle with trees.

The artist most affectionately identified with the Kentucky River is a painter, the American impressionist Paul Sawyier (1865–1917). Growing up in Frankfort, Sawyier was drawn to the hills and creeks of the Kentucky River country. Receiving most of his formal training at the Cincinnati Art Academy, Sawyier set up a studio and supported himself for a time in Cincinnati doing crayon portraits. His father persuaded him to return to Frankfort to work as a hemp salesman for the Kentucky River Mill, but in 1887 he gave up the job to paint landscapes and river scenes about the capital. He later studied watercolor at the Arts Students League in New York and also returned to Cincinnati where he worked under Frank Duveneck, a well-known portrait painter from Kentucky. Skilled in working with oils, pastels, and copperplate etchings, Sawyier's characteristic medium was watercolor.

Cascading water of Jessamine Creek.

Though Sawyier painted Frankfort street scenes and a few portraits, he is best known for his landscapes, which show the Kentucky River and its tributaries. In 1908 he bought a houseboat, which he used both as a studio and living quarters. From 1908 to the fall of 1913 he spent most of his time on the Kentucky River, tying up at High Bridge and Camp Nelson between Locks Seven and Eight where he painted many views of the Palisades. At High Bridge he made friends with the ferry operator, often staying at his home during spates of bad weather. Sawyier became well-known in the neighborhood and was called "the artist who lives in a houseboat" or "the river artist." At High Bridge and Camp Nelson he was often visited by a sweetheart, friends, and his few patrons. The central Kentucky newspapers cultivated romantic image of Sawyier living aboard his houseboat:

> [H]e lives through all the seasons of the year in a houseboat —or a 'shanty boat' as the natives dub it—on the Kentucky River. He is generally anchored at or near High Bridge, where all his work is done.

Sometimes he painted from nature, but often he used photographs as an aid to his compositions. After living five years on the river, he moved from Kentucky to Brooklyn, New York, in 1913 to live with his sister and later moved upstate to the Catskills where in 1917 he died at age fifty-two after suffering a heart attack. In 1923 his remains were returned to Frankfort to the same high bluff where Boone lies, overlooking the state capitol and his beloved river. His legacy is assured in the prints of Palisades and river scenes that decorate the homes and offices of thousands of Kentuckians.

The beauty of the Palisades finally lies in its combination of genders. The river's grace and subtlety, as seen in Sawyier's paintings, present a feminine principle of light and color, an elusive but active element of motion and change that the

Sunrise on the Kentucky River,
Jessamine and Garrard Counties.

*Fog enshrouds fields at dawn,
Jessamine County.*

Buckeye butterfly.

impressionist seeks to embody in paint. Seen close at hand, the slopes render trees and plants of almost indescribable beauty: ferns and wildflowers along the moist facings, a patchwork of moss or lichen on overhanging rocks, the elegant white tracings of sycamore limbs in the bottoms during winter.

Yet from a distance the stone facings have a masculine aspect: stoic, Roman, architectural. Auguste Rodin, endlessly translating stone into robust form, would have marveled at the natural sculptings of the Palisades. Viewed from the river, it is easy to imagine the columns and crags as a muster of old farmers, shoulder to shoulder, presiding over the valley—gray, rough-hewn, weathered, mutely assertive. Neither as flamboyant as flatboaters of the legendary Mike Fink variety nor as single-mindedly industrious as the Shakers, they call up images of the faceless tobacco farmers, loggers, steamboat pilots, and frontier hunters who prospered and died along the river's banks. At an aesthetic level, this alloy of masculine and feminine mutations accounts for the visual appeal of the Palisades—the interplay of rock and water, fixity and motion, wildness and filigree.

The Palisades is first among the "curiosities" that Harry Toulmin cites in his *A Description of Kentucky in North America*:

> The banks or rather precipices of Kentucky and Dick's rivers, are to be rekoned [*sic*] among the natural curiosities of this country. Here the astonished eye beholds 3 or 400 feet of solid perpindicular [*sic*] rock, in some parts of the lime-stone kind, and in others of fine white marble, curiously chequered with strata of astonishing regularity.

The impulse to paint and photograph the Palisades derives from a common desire to memorialize the encounter between the human and the wild. "Art," as Guy Davenport, a writer and artist living in Lexington said, "is always the replacement of indifference by attention." Difficult, sometimes dangerous, to shoot, Adam Jones's photographs in this book are feats of attention that focus on what is easily missed or simply too vast to assimilate except through framed visual images. They are an extension of the pictorial impulse to commemorate what is grand and picturesque in our natural environment, a necessary counterbalance to the sometimes tawdry grandeur of our built environment. As the poet Ezra Pound wrote, "Grass"—and by extension trees, rocks, and clouds—"is nowhere out of place."

Crab spider on black-eyed Susan.

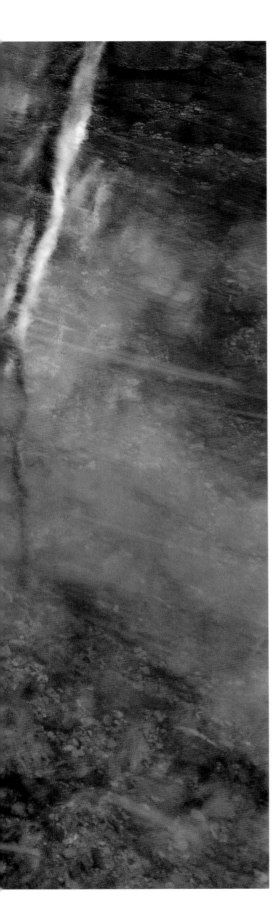

Above: A great egret.

Opposite: A clear, still pool in
Jessamine Creek reflects trees.

Navigation

From the beginning, traffic on the Kentucky was heavy and diverse. Nicholas Cresswell, an Englishman, was one of a party of fourteen on the river from May 22 to June 4, 1775. At a time when the region now known as Kentucky had very few settlers, he encountered thirteen canoes, all heading to the Ohio and back upriver to Wheeling, Fort Pitt, or Redstone on the Monongahela. Many of these early parties were surveyors seeking the most desirable sites for patent holders whose service in the French and Indian War entitled them to land in the western country. During the summer of 1773 brothers James and Robert McAfee and

surveyor Hancock Taylor were the first to plot land on the banks of the Kentucky, which they called the Levisa. Entries in their journals, published in the 1905 *Wood-McAfee Memorial,* indicate that they traveled all the way to the forks of the Kentucky before returning to Virginia. James's entry of July 31, 1773, reports: "We left crooked Creek where we got our lands surveyed and set off up Cantucky river for home… This evening very wet. We came about 7 miles, part of it through cane breaks, to a large creek; camped that night under a rock at the foot of a high cedar hill." Robert's entry for the same day gives a sense of the harsh conditions under which the party performed its work: "We lay all night by the side of the river under the very high rocks to shelter the rain, & dry our things—for it was exceeding wet."

The perils of traveling overland, which included hostile Indians and wild animals, were great. Before they reached Virginia, members of the party nearly starved in the mountains before fortuitously bringing down a bear.

The history of navigation on the Kentucky moves through several stages. First and longest was the period of dugout canoes used both by Native Americans and whites. With the era of settlement and trade came the flatboat, constructed to go only one way—with the current. Their lumber, when they reached their destination, was then salvaged for houses and outbuildings. A third step in the progression was the keelboat, a larger and more elaborate vessel, capable of carrying more substantial freight. It went downriver with the current—sometimes all the way to New Orleans—and then was literally pulled back upstream by the laborious process of poling, often supplemented by "cordelling"—tying the vessel to overhanging trees and painstakingly drawing it upstream. To lessen the drudgery, crude sails were sometimes raised on open stretches of water like the Ohio.

In the early years of the nineteenth century, steam power for transportation by water became a reality, and by 1816 passenger steamboats were paddling up the river as far as water levels would allow. This innovation opened the rivers for commerce, providing the first reliable means by which goods and people could be conveyed upstream as well as down. Though low pools, snags, and deadheads were formidable obstacles, steam power provided the technological breakthrough that opened the backcountry before the advent of the railroads. Over the ensuing decades, boat builders along the Kentucky and Ohio Rivers sought to reduce the drafts of these floating hotels and at the same time deepen the channels in which they floated.

Lock Seven in late winter.

Almost overnight the hill country witnessed a revolution in conveyance because steamboats increasingly penetrated the Palisades region as far as the Forks at Beattyville and beyond. The passenger list of the *Blue Wing,* the most famous of the Kentucky River steamboats and similar vessels, was a roll call of the most prominent leaders in the state—John J. Crittenden, Cassius Clay, Henry Clay, John C. Breckinridge, Robert Breckinridge, Governors Robert Letcher and Charles Morehead, and

Palisades along the Dix River in spring.

Trees arch over the Dix River.

A boater on the Kentucky River at dawn.

A spring morning on the Kentucky River.

Overhanging branches and mirrored
shoreline along the Kentucky River.

many others. Added to these numbers were wealthy planters and their families who came by river up from the deep South to visit the spas such as Graham Springs at Harrodsburg. They came to enjoy the healthful waters, to escape yellow fever and the oppressive Southern heat, and to socialize. Until the Civil War, whole families of out-of-staters collected at these resorts to entertain themselves and "take the waters." An added attraction for travelers to Graham Springs, just eight miles from Shaker Landing, was the beauty of the Palisades. Starting in 1845, the *Blue Wing* made regular runs twice a week from Louisville on the Ohio to Carrollton and then up the Kentucky to such destinations as Frankfort, Woodford Landing (at Clifton), Oregon (nineteen miles farther upstream), Munday's Landing (opposite the mouth of Shawnee Run and just downstream from Shaker Landing), and "all intermediate points" on the river. Because of low water levels, navigation above Frankfort was possible only for about half the year.

To those closer to the headwaters, steamboats were something of a curiosity. In his *The Kentucky,* historian Thomas Clark recounts a story in which unusually high water permitted the *Blue Wing II,* captained by the legendary Harry Innes Todd, to steam far upriver nearly to Irvine and sometimes as far as the three forks at Beattyville. At Irvine he caused a sensation because many there had never seen a steamboat. On the morning of March 15, 1846, he was greeted by crowds along the banks that came to gawk at the floating palace. But not all the watchers were entertained. One amazed onlooker leveled his squirrel rifle at, as Clark puts it, "this beautiful specimen of naval architecture." Witnessing the fire and black smoke shooting from the twin stacks, this patriot was about to shoot it as he would some ravaging beast, when one of his neighbors saw the danger and deflected his fire. The unrepentant defender of his homeland reportedly wailed, "Do you call that a steamboat? Well, she stood a smart chance of getting shot; I was going to give it to her 'tween the horns'."

Despite these occasional "inconveniences," for the first time farmers in the Bluegrass and eastern Kentucky had an affordable and fairly reliable means to get their produce to distant markets. Hams, tobacco, corn (fermented and unfermented), butter, hempen products like bagging and rope, and other goods reliably flowed to exotic places downriver. Trade along the Kentucky and Ohio Rivers thrived.

Steamboat building also became a booming industry along the river, at such places as Steamboat Bottom near Frankfort. One of the earliest steamboats was constructed during the spring of 1816 in the shadow of the Palisades in Jessamine County. Leaving from the mouth of Hickman Creek on April 21st, it transported a load of goods to New Orleans.

From the earliest days it was clear that the key to using the river lay in improvements that would increase its navigability and safety. As early as 1792 — the year of Kentucky's statehood — improving the Kentucky was discussed by the state legislature, though active efforts to improve the channel were not made until the advent of steamboats on the Kentucky in 1816. The biggest problem, which especially restricted river traffic upriver, was low pools during the summer months. By the 1830s, when the traffic in steamboats, flatboats, and log rafts considerably expanded river commerce, the Kentucky legislature authorized studies of a system of locks. Bids were eventually let, and construction of the locks began. In 1840 the first steamboat locked upstream to Frankfort, and commerce on the lower Kentucky increased substantially. Eventually and after many delays, five locks between the mouth at Carrollton and upriver at Clifton in Woodford County were completed in 1844. During the Civil War the Union army made use of the system to transport supplies upriver to Camps Nelson and Dick Robinson, though maintenance of the locks was neglected. By war's end in 1865 they were badly in need of repair.

Relief came in 1880 when the U.S. government assumed jurisdiction over the river following a congressional survey of the river under the Rivers and Harbors Act. Lock gates were repaired, and the lower four locks were reopened in 1882. By 1886, when the fifth was reopened at Clifton, there had been a resurgence of river trade. In response to political pressure upriver, an experimental dam called a bear trap was built at Beattyville in 1883. The dam had two movable gates. Sixty feet wide, they were to be opened when there was sufficient water to carry boats and rafts downriver on a "tide," a rush of water created when water behind the lock was released. According to Charles Parrish, historian at the U.S. Army Corps of Engineers office in Louisville, the experiment was a disaster. So rapid was the release of dammed up water flowing through the chutes that the descent caused wrecks and near drownings as crewmen, in fear of their lives, jumped from the vessels.

Between 1880 and 1917 the Corps of Engineers completed a system of fourteen locks from the mouth of the Kentucky to Beattyville, creating a slackwater depth of six feet for nearly 260 miles. By this time railroad service in eastern Kentucky had substantially cut into the shipment of coal and timber from the region by water. In recent years commercial navigation on the river has slumped, replaced by pleasure boating. There has been no commercial traffic north of Lock Four at Frankfort since the late 1970s, and now the state-run Kentucky River Authority, created in 1986 by the Kentucky General Assembly as an entity to receive ownership of the abandoned lock and dam system, controls the whole system.

Almost as colorful as the steamboating era is the time when rafts of logs floated out of the eastern Kentucky timberlands, a practice that began during the early days of settlement and accelerated in the last quarter of the nineteenth century. From 1875 on, thousands of acres of virgin hardwoods in eastern Kentucky were clearcut and toppled or dragged to the river where log rafts were formed to convey them to mills in Frankfort and Louisville where millions of board feet were converted into building materials. So massive were these rafts and so unpredictable was the depth of the river that they could be moved only on the fall and spring tides. The hearty raftsmen armed themselves against individuals who often stoned or even shot at them from the Palisades or bridges, and then the thirsty hillmen unwound in the saloons and pleasure houses of North Frankfort's Crawfish Bottom.

According to the late Bill Kephart, formerly a captain of the *Dixie Belle,* loggers in the eastern mountains would cut, trim, and roll their logs to the river banks and wait for high water. Each log would be branded with the owner's particular identification. When the rise came, the logs would be rolled into the water and "roar down the river," to be picked up, or caught, at the numerous sawmills along the way. The mills used log booms—usually of cottonwood because it floated high in the water —to trap the logs so they could be pulled out. As they were processed, a notation of the brand was penciled into a ledger. One such sawmill was at Shaker Landing, where logs were dragged out of the water on an inclined plane, a runway laid perpendicular to the water so logs could be slid up the mud banks. During the summer the logmen descended in their canoes or pirogues and would go to each sawmill for payment. "I'm J.D.," the logger would say. "How many of my logs did you pull?" "Now can you believe that?" Bill Kephart said. "Isn't that beautiful?"

Summer foliage and waterfall,
Jessamine Gorge.

A pond at dawn,
Mercer County.

A Sunday Morning Excursion

On a Sunday morning in late October I joined a nature hike in the Palisades area at Pleasant Hill in Mercer County. Don Pelly, the biologist who coordinates these activities, was accompanied by Tom Edwards, the district wildlife biologist for central Kentucky. To a group of fifteen or twenty of us, Tom described the savanna-like environment as recorded by the first whites more than 200 years earlier—the deep-rooted buffalo grass, Indian grass, and bluestem on which bison, deer, and elk browsed, and the bobcats, gray wolves, and black bears that preyed in turn on the bison, deer, and elk.

After crossing a stone stile and U.S. 68, we passed through an upland field along the 1860s road that descends to Shaker Ferry. Along the way our guides described the flora and fauna, moving from the introduced species of bush honeysuckle, acanthus (tree of heaven), and osage orange (with softball-size fruit that one schoolgirl referred to as "monkey brains") to less disturbed

Spider awaiting prey.

habitats as we went down the narrow road blasted and dug from the rock facings. Don Pelly, who has studied the area for more than a decade, estimated that about 30 percent of the plants that now grow in the gorge area are non-native. The Palisades, however, contain a higher percentage of native plants than almost any other area in the region. Remote, too steep for pasturage or cultivation, the rocky cliffs and slopes are both a botanical museum and an incubator for plant species that have existed there for thousands of years. Long before the advent of humans, the river valley has served as a "travel corridor" for animal and plant species. Just as the river has served as the means by which Shaker deacons distributed packets of seeds all over the South, it also has served that purpose for eons by natural processes.

Though the hillsides have been cut over, second and third growths give a fair representation of the mixed mesophytic forests that mantled the Palisades when the early settlers entered the river basin. Slow declines of hard mast, mostly beechnuts and hickory nuts, have diminished small mammal populations, and some tree species such as the American chestnut have virtually disappeared. Other plants are threatened or rare. *Draba ramoissima,* an inconspicuous flowering plant of the mustard family that grows at the base of the moist facings, is described as rare in Kentucky. Yellowwood, *Cladrastis lutea,* a handsome, gray-barked tree with pinnate leaves and drooping panicles of white flowers was also pointed out as rare. Though seldom seen in the wild, it is increasingly common as an ornamental.

The south-facing cliffs support several varieties of ferns, including falling and Christmas ferns, as well as early saxifrage and the prickly pear cactus that is native to the area. We were informed that the Shakers planted mulberry trees in an attempt to create a silkworm industry on the 5,000 acres they once owned.

Tom Edwards pulled from his pocket the cast of a bobcat's paw print, pointing out the characteristic rounded pads. At other points he sounded a crow call and a plaintive imitation of a dying rabbit to see what avian predators might be attracted.

Along the way Don Pelly pointed out the uses of plants we happened on. The sassafras seedlings along the fencerow, for instance, made buckets and pails. Beans of the black locusts provided a kind of coffee. In this century, the downy innards of milkweed pods, called kapok, became stuffing for life jackets. As we sat eating a box lunch at the ferry, we watched some birders trying to aid a red-tailed hawk whose wing had been injured. Sitting on stone foundations at Shaker Landing, nearly enveloped by the Palisades's vertical thrust of lichen-covered stone and fall plumage, we eyed a trio of buzzards that wheeled high above the gorge and sensed the magic of this place where moving water endlessly gnaws at rock. I reflected on our own insignificance amid the evidence of so much elapsed time.

*A cascade in spring,
near Pollys Bend.*

Left: Buckeye butterfly on a bull thistle, Mercer County.

Opposite: Alternate-leaved wingstem, ironweed, and sneezewood in late summer, Garrard County.

The road to Shaker Landing in autumn, Mercer County.

The return route was an earlier stagecoach road, narrower and more dangerous, that twisted around the facings close by the later road where slabs of stone still showed the drill holes of the Irish laborers who helped the Shakers build it. As we ascended into an overgrown field, we passed the remnants of a stone chimney thought to be the remains of the Shaker toll house. From this pile of stones we could construct images of the toll keeper exacting a fee from each farmer who passed that way to cross the river or to ship goods on the packets at dockside. The parking lot at the village reintroduced us to our own century.

Leaving, cased in metal, my daughter and I again descended to the river, this time down U.S. 68. Through a fringe of trees, we caught glimpses of the gray buttresses that had formed along the waterway during a time whose glimmerings we could divine at best through the abstractions of number and the tenuous reconstructions of science. At the base of this turret of trees and rocks stand several summer houses built above the floodplain on stilts or pilings. They are dwarfed by high walls of stone that form a chasm, with its own light, its own narrow corridor where dawn over the stony summit comes later and darkness sooner. Over the railing, beneath us, the river flows invisibly, the glazed mica of its surface unruffled as a pond. Logless, boatless, its current chafes away at the rock, undetectably whisking off bits toward the Gulf of Mexico, the task of its waters being to bring high things low.

Magnificent and wonderfully flawed edifices of sea bones tower above us, aloof and ever apart, their crannies tenanted by birds and a few sure-footed quadrupeds. Crossing the Brooklyn Bridge and beginning the spiral upward to follow the backroads through Troy to Versailles and on to Frankfort, I felt the stolid presence of nature's masonry, a stone citadel neither plumb nor square, but random, self-justifying, almost casually sublime. Having crossed the bridge, we wound again up through a groin of carved rock toward the sunny uplands that would widen the sky and light our way home.

Frost on cinquefoil.

Junction of Jessamine Creek and the Kentucky River.

A houseboat anchored on the
Kentucky River near Brooklyn Bridge.

*Palisades mirrored
on the Kentucky River.*

Fire pinks.

Technical Information

The photographs in this book were made with a Pentax 67 system, using 220 film and Pentax SMC lenses of 45mm, 55mm, 90mm, 135mm, 200mm, and 300mm. In addition, many images were made with a 35mm format with Pentax PZ-Ip cameras and an assortment of Pentax lenses from 24mm to 600mm. All exposures were calculated with in-camera meters on Fujichrome Professional 100 and Velvia films. In some cases a polarizing, slight warming filter or graduated neutral density filter was used. The support system consisted of a Gitzo 320 tripod with a Bogen three-way-tilt pan head.

Many of the photographs were taken from a motorboat or from ledges where I was secured by a rope. All images from the motorboat were handheld using ISO 100 film pushed one stop for extra speed. In every case, the scene was rendered as truthfully as possible to the experience.

Special thanks to the Louisville companies of Whittenberg Photographic for supplying film and Omni Lab for providing all the film processing.

Bibliography

Belue, Ted. *The Long Hunt: Death of the Buffalo East of the Mississippi,* Stackpole Books, Mechanicsburg, Pennsylvania, 1996.

Chinn, George Morgan. *Kentucky: Settlers and Statehood, 1750–1800,* Kentucky State Historical Society, Frankfort, Kentucky, 1975.

Clark, Thomas D. *The Kentucky,* University Press of Kentucky, Lexington, Kentucky, 1992.

Clark, Thomas D., and F. Gerald Ham. *Pleasant Hill and its Shakers,* Shakertown Press, Pleasant Hill, Kentucky, 1968.

Coleman, J. Winston, Jr. *Steamboats on the Kentucky River,* Winburn Press, Lexington, Kentucky, 1960.

Cresswell, Nicholas. *The Journal of Nicholas Cresswell, 1774–1777,* 2d ed., Dial Press, New York, New York, 1924.

Curry, Howard. *High Bridge, A Pictorial History,* Feeback Printing, Inc., Lexington, Kentucky, 1983.

Filson, John. *The Discovery and Settlement of Kentucky,* facsimilie edition, Readex Microprint, 1966.

Grier, Bill. "The Five Lives of the Kentucky River," (unpublished paper) 1996.

Jessamine County Historical and Genealogical Society, Inc., *History of Jessamine County,* Taylor Publishing Company, Dallas, Texas, 1993.

Jillson, Willard Rouse. *The Kentucky,* The State Journal, Frankfort, Kentucky, 1945.

Jones, Arthur F. *The Art of Paul Sawyier,* University Press of Kentucky, Lexington, Kentucky, 1976.

Kentucky Rivers Assessment. Kentucky Division of Water, Frankfort, Kentucky, 1992.

Kleber, John E., ed. *The Kentucky Encyclopedia,* University Press of Kentucky, Lexington, Kentucky, 1992.

McFarland, Arthur C. *Behind the Scenery in Kentucky,* Kentucky Geological Survey, Lexington, Kentucky, 1958.

Michaux, André. "Journal of Travels into Kentucky, July 15, 1793–April 11,1796," in *Early Western Travels,* Vol. 3. 1748–1846, Reuben G. Thwaites, ed., Arthur H. Clark Company, Cleveland, Ohio, 1904.

Neal, Julia. *The Shakers of Kentucky,* University Press of Kentucky, Lexington, Kentucky, 1982.

Parrish, Charles E. "Navigation Development on the Kentucky River," in *The Army Engineer,* Vol. 3, No. 1, Army Engineer Association, March–April 1995.

Sears, Richard. "John G. Fee, Camp Nelson, and Kentucky Blacks, 1864–65," in *Register of the Kentucky Historical Society,* Vol. 85, No. 1, Winter 1987.

Toulmin, Harry. "A Description of Kentucky, 1792," in *A Transylvanian Trilogy,* Willard Rouse Jillson, ed., Kentucky State Historical Society, Frankfort, Kentucky, reprint 1932.

Verhoeff, Mary. *The Kentucky River Navigation,* Filson Club Publications No. 28, John P. Morton & Company, Louisville, Kentucky, 1917.

Wharton, Mary E., and Roger W. Barbour. *Bluegrass Land and Life,* University Press of Kentucky, Lexington, Kentucky, 1991.

Wood-McAfee Memorial, Louisville, Kentucky, 1905

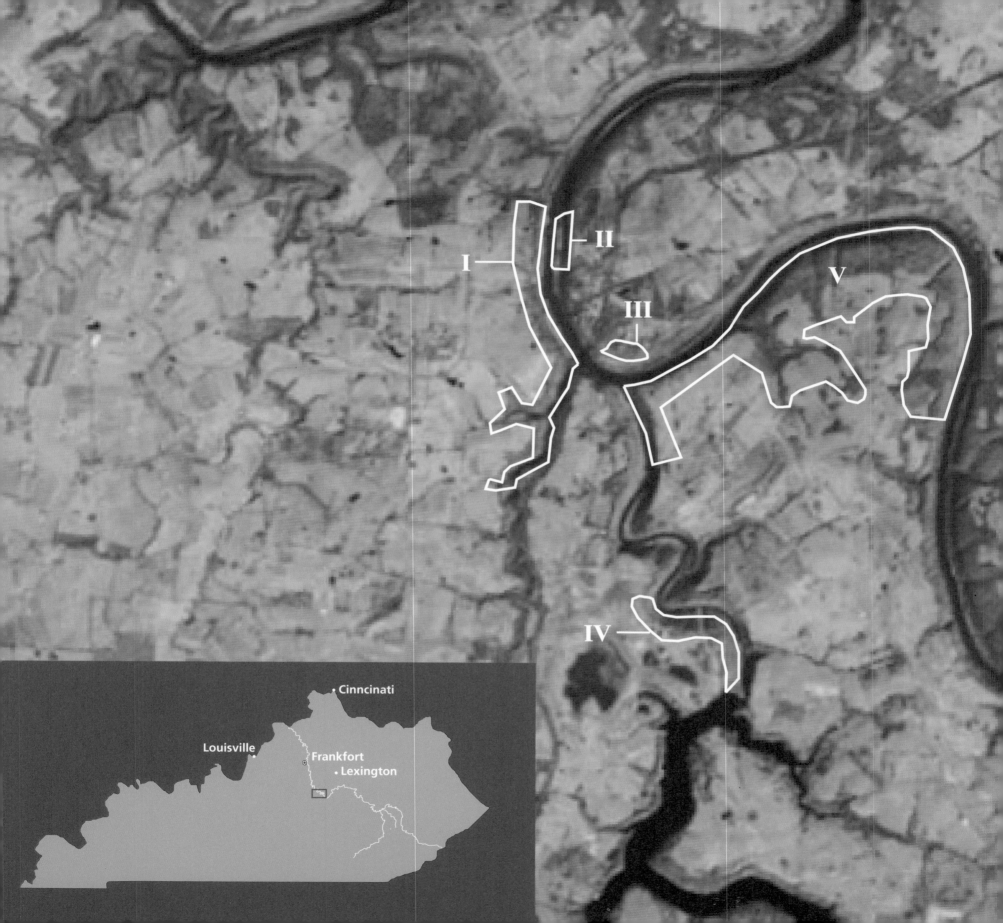